WHAT
𝔖alem 𝔇ames
COOKED

WHAT
𝔖𝔞𝔩𝔢𝔪 𝔇𝔞𝔪𝔢𝔰
COOKED

Being *A Choice Collection of Recipes* wherein is shewn how THE DELECTABLE PRACTICE of the SALEM DAMES from the year 1683, to 1730, until 1800 and 1900, may be restored with pleasure to those desirous of experiencing *The* DELIGHTS *of their* COOKERY, together with A Few Housekeeping *Hints* and Numerous *Appropriate Quotations*.

Compiled and Published
by
THE BOARD OF MANAGERS
of the School

with a cover design by
ROSS TURNER

DERBY SQUARE
◆PRESS◆
The Wicked Good Books Publishing House

COPYRIGHT 1910 BY THE BOARD OF MANAGERS OF
THE ESTHER C. MACK INDUSTRIAL SCHOOL, SALEM

CONTENTS

"The Compleat Cook's Guide"
1683

"The Frugal Housewife
OR
COMPLETE WOMAN COOK
WHEREIN
The *Art of Dressing* all sorts of VIANDS
with CLEANLINESS, DECENCY and
ELEGANCE is Explained"
1730

Our Grandmothers' Cook Books
1800

Our Own Cook Books
1900

FROM
"The Compleat Cook's Guide"
1683

A BILL OF FARE *for Midsomer*

First Course
1. A Neats-tongue and Colliflowers
2. A Fore Quarter of Lamb
3. A Chicken-Pye
4. Boylee Pigeons
5. A couple of Stewed Rabbits
6. A Breast of Veal Roasted

Second Course
1. An Artichoak Pye
2. A Venison Pasty
3. Lobsters and Salmon
4. A Dish of Pease
5. A Gooseberry-Tart
6. A Dish of Strawberries

To Make a CHICKEN-PYE

AFTER you have Trust your chickens, then break their Legs and Breast-bones, and raise your crust of the best Paste, lay them in a Coffin close together, with their bodies full of butter, then lay upon and underneath them, Currans, great Raisins, Pruans, Cinnamon, Sugar, whole Mace and Sugar, whole Mace and Salt; then cover all with good store of butter, and so bake it; then pour into it white-wine, rose-water, sugar, cinnamon, and vinegar mixt together, with Yolks of two or three Eggs beaten amongst it, and so serve it.

To Make a HEDG-HOG PUDDING

PUT some Raisins of the Sun into a deep wooden Dish, and then take some grated bread, and one pint of sweet Cream, three yolks of Eggs, with two of the whites, and some Beef Suet, grated Nutmeg and Salt, then sweeten it with sugar, and temper it all well together, and so lay it into the dish upon the Raisins, then tye a cloath about the dish, and boyl it in Beef-broth and when you take it up lay it in a pewter Dish, with the Raisins uppermost, and then

What Salem Dames Cooked

ſtick blanched Almonds very thick upon the pudding, then melt ſome butter and pour it upon the pudding, then ſtrew ſome ſugar about the diſh, and ſerve it.

To Make a Pye with Pippins

PARE your pippins, and cut out the cores, then make your Coffin of cruſt, take a good handful of Quinces ſliced and lay at the bottom, then lay your pippins a top, and fill the holes where the core was taken out with Syrup of Quinces, and put into every Pippin a piece of Orangado, then pour on the top Syrup of Quinces, then put in Sugar, and ſo cloſe it up, let it be very well baked, for it will aſk much ſoaking, eſpecially the Quinces.

To Make an Orangado Pye

MAKE a handſome thin Coffin, with hot butter'd Paſte, ſlice fine Orangado, and put over the bottom of it, then take some pippins; and cut every one into eight parts, and lay them in alſo upon the Orangado, then pour ſome ſyrup of Orangado, and Sugar on the top, and ſo make it up, and bake it and ſerve it up with ſugar ſcraped on it.

Typical Prices in early New England

1632-1650	1700	1740
4 eggs, 1d.	Salmon, 1d. lb.	"Butcher's meat: beef, mutton, lamb, veal, averaged 2d. a lb.; the very best, 6d; turkeys, 2s.; a twelve pound cod, 2d.; salmon about 1d. a lb.; large lobsters, 3 half pence; butter, 3d. The diet of large towns and affluent people."
1 qt. milk, 1d.	Cider, 6 to 7s. gal.	
1 lb. butter, 6d.	Turnips, 1s. 3d. bu.	
1 qt. beer, 6d.	Apples, 10s. bu.	
1 lb. cheese, 5d.	Cinnamon, 14s. lb.	
1 bu. corn, 6s.	Cloves, 20s. lb.	
1 warming pan, 5s. 6d.	Nutmegs, 20s. lb.	
1 pair spectacles, 2s.	Bohea tea, 25s. lb.	
1 pair andirons, 10s.	Snuff, 16s. lb.	
Apples, 6 to 8s. bu.	Molasses, 13d. gal.	
Beef, 3d. lb.	N. E. rum, 4s. 10d. gal.	
Pork, 4d. lb.	Butter, 18d. lb.	

FROM
"The Frugal Housewife"
1730

To Make Good Wigs

TO four Pounds of fine Flower, take one Pound of good Butter, half a Pound of fine Sugar, a handful of Carraway Comfits or Seeds, and a little Rose-Water; work it up with a Pint of good Ale-yeast strained and as much milk as will wet them warmed: put in some Ginger, and work them up light and set them in a warm Place to rise: make them in Bigness as you think fit, and bake them on Iron Plates in a quick Oven: they will be done in half a quarter of an Hour.

To Carbonade a Breast of Mutton

TAKE a breast of mutton, half bone it, knick it across. Season it with pepper and salt, then broil it before the fire whilst it be enough, Strinkling it over with bread crumbs: let the same be a little Gravy and butter and a few shred capers: put it upon the dish with the mutton. Garnish it with horse-radish and pickles. This is proper for a side-dish at noon or a bottom dish at night.

> *"You shall see first the large and chief*
> *Foundation of your feast, fat beef;*
> *With upper stories, mutton, veal*
> *And bacon, which makes full the meal,*
> *With several dishes standing by*
> *As, here a custard, there a pie*
> *And here, all tempting, frumenty."* HERRICK

Burnt Cream

BOIL a stick of cinnamon in a pint of cream, four eggs well beat, leaving out the whites; boil the cream and thicken it with the eggs as for a custard: then put it in your

What Salem Dames Cooked

dish and put over it half a pound of loaf sugar beat and seared: heat a fire-shovel red hot and hold it over the top till the sugar be brown. So serve it up.

For the Sick

PANOLA, made in five minutes. Set a little water on the fire with a glass of white wine, some sugar and a scrape of nutmeg or lemon peel. Meanwhile grate some crumbs of bread; the moment the mixture boils up keeping it still on the fire, put the crumbs in and let it boil as fast as it can. When of a proper thickness just to drink take it off.

A Most Pleasant Drink

PUT a teacupfull of cranberries into a cup of water and mash them. In the meantime boil 2 quarts and a pint of water with one large spoonful of oatmeal and a very large bit of lemon peel. Then add the cranberries and as much fine Lisbon sugar as shall leave a smart.

Another

AS above, but instead of a glass of wine, put in a teaspoonful of rum and a bit of butter, sugar as above. This is a most pleasant mess!!

Shrewsbury Cakes

SIFT 1 pound of sugar, some pounded cinnamon, and a nutmeg grated with three lbs. of flour, the finest sort; add a little rose-water to 3 eggs well beaten, and mix them with the flour, etc.; then pour into it as much butter melted as will make it a good thickness and roll out. Mould it well, roll thin, cut into such shapes as you like.

"Small cheer and great welcome makes a merry feast."
COMEDY OF ERRORS

FROM
Our Grandmother's Cook Book
1800

Cookery means the knowledge of Medea and of Circe and of Helen and the Queen of Sheba. It means the knowledge of all herbs and fruits and balms and spices, and all that is healing and sweet in the fields and groves and savory in meats. It means carefulness and inventiveness and willingness and readiness of appliances. It means the economy of your grandmothers and the science of the modern chemist; it means much testing and no wasting; it means English thoroughness and French art, and Arabian hospitality; and in fine, it means that you are to be perfectly and always ladies—loaf-givers.

RUSKIN

To Make a TRIFLE

COVER the bottom of a dish or bowl with Naples biscuits broke in pieces, macaroons in halves and ratafia cakes. Just wet them through with sack: then make a good boiled custard not too thick and when cold pour it over, then put a syllabub over that. You may garnish with ratafia cakes, currant-jelly and flowers.

POUND CAKE

1¼ lbs. sugar, 1¼ lbs. flour, 1 lb. butter. Eggs same weight as sugar—a little nutmeg, mace. (S.P.)

DARBYSHIRE PUDDING

MIX gradually 2 tablespoons of flour with a pint of milk. Boil till thick, when cold add 3 oz. butter beaten to a cream—1¼ oz. sugar, rind of a lemon grated. Yolks of 5 eggs, and whites of these, a little salt. Mix very thoroughly. Line a shallow dish with pastry and fill with the mixture. Bake in a quick oven. This is nicest eaten cold. MRS. DEVEREUX

"Now good digestion wait on appetite and health on both."
SHAKSPEARE

What Salem Dames Cooked

Apple Fritters

Pare and core the apples, cut in slices ⅓ of an inch thick, dip in batter and fry 6 minutes in boiling fat. For the Batter: 1 pt. flour, 1 pt. milk, 1 tablespoon butter, 1 teaspoon salt, 2 eggs. Beat the eggs light, add salt and milk to them, pour this mixture into the flour, beat until smooth and soft. For Sauce: A heap of granulated sugar was placed on one plate and moistened with wine or cider.

Meg Merrilies Pottage

Take 1 partridge, 1 quail, 1 rabbit, 2 lbs. venison, 6 cloves, 4 blades mace, small pinch cayenne and of black pepper, salt to taste, ½ wineglass lemon juice, 2 small onions, 2 stalks celery, a little parsley, 1 very small carrot and parsnip, a little marjoram, 4 potatoes cut thin and put in one hour before done; the rest to be boiled all day.

> *"All human history attests*
> *That happiness for man—the hungry sinner!—*
> *Since Eve ate apples, much depends on dinner."* — BYRON

White Currant Shrub

Strip the fruit and prepare in a jar as for jelly; strain the juice, if white put two quarts to one gallon of rum and two pounds of lump sugar, strain through a jelly bag. (1807)

Bannuch Cake

Take 3 pints of milk scalded. 4 eggs—little salt with saleratus—as much fine Indian meal as will make a batter a little more stiff than for griddle cakes. Pour into pans or muffin rings, bake on a griddle.

> *"We may live without friends, we may live without books,*
> *But civilized man cannot live without cooks."* — OWEN MEREDITH

Our Grandmother's Cook Book

CORN PONE

TAKE 1 pint corn meal, 2 eggs, dessert-spoonful of lard and a little salt. Pour enough boiling water on to melt the lard, then add sufficient milk to make it thin enough to make a smooth crust. Bake in little pans.   MARY DONALDSON

ENGLISH HUNTING BEEF

A ROUND of beef weighing about 20 lbs. Take 1 oz. of cloves, 1 oz. allspice, 2 nutmegs, ¼ lb. saltpetre, 2 teacups brown sugar, and 2 teacups salt. Let all these be reduced to powder and mixed well together. Rub them very thoroughly into the beef, and last of all, rub in a teacupful of molasses. Turn and rub the beef thoroughly every day for 11 or 12 days. Before baking wash off the loose spice, and roll it in a crash roller, binding very tightly. Put it in a tin pan with a pint of cold water, and a little shred suet strewed over the top of the beef. Put paper over the beef and over the edge of the pan; and upon this put a crust of rye meal and warm water laid loosely over the whole, particularly over the edges to keep in the steam, and bake; if in an iron oven about four hours. If a brick oven be used, it should be quite hot, and the beef kept in until the oven cools. When taken from the oven let the beef remain in the pan till cold. The gravy strained and bottled will keep some time, and is nice either with the beef or used to flavor beefsteak, or any stewed fish. Through the days when the beef is preparing for cooking, I generally keep it in a large brown earthen pan, with another pan turned over it. A yard of crash, split into four and joined together, makes a roller sufficiently long.   MRS. GUSTAVUS TUCKERMAN

YELLOW GINGERBREAD

2 lbs. flour, 1½ lbs. sugar, 1½ lbs. butter, ¼ lb. yellow ginger after it is sifted, 1 wineglass of brandy.

What Salem Dames Cooked

Zanzibar Gingerbread

12 lbs. flour, 8 lbs. sugar, 6 lbs. butter, 18 eggs, ½ pint rosewater, teacupful ginger, 6 teaspoons saleratus.

"Ate last piece of mother's gingerbread to-day." — ITEM FROM SEAMAN'S DIARY

Whip Syllabub

1 qt. cream, not very thick, 1 pt. sack, whites of 3 eggs, juice of 2 lemons, sweeten it to your taste. Put it in a broad earthen pan and with a whisk whip it up, and as the froth rises take it off with a spoon and put it into a sieve that the cream may run out.

> *"If thou hast found a honey comb*
> *Eat thou not all, but taste on some;*
> *For if thou eat'st it to excess*
> *That sweetness turns to loathsomeness.*
> *Taste it to temper — then 'twill be*
> *Marrow and manna unto thee."*   HERRICK

Wedding Cake

10 lbs. sugar, 1½ lbs. butter, 9½ lbs. flour, 7 dozen eggs, 9 lbs. currants, 9 lbs. raisins, 9 lbs. almonds, 4 lbs. citron, ½ lb. nutmeg, ¼ lb. cinnamon, 1 oz. mace, 1 oz. cloves, 1 pint brandy, 1 coffee cup molasses, 9 drops oil of lemon.

MRS. H. GODDARD

Election Cake

6 lbs. flour, 2 lbs. sugar, 1 lb. butter, 12 eggs, 1 quart of milk, 1 pint of yeast, mace.   (S. P.) SALTONSTALL

Salem Pudding

3 cups flour, 1 cup milk, 1 cup molasses, 1 cup chopped suet, 1 cup raisins chopped fine, ½ teaspoon saleratus or 1 teaspoon soda put into the molasses. Boil in a pudding boiler four to five hours.

Our Grandmother's Cook Book

Molly Saunders' Gingerbread

Lower Shelf: 3½ lbs. flour, 1 lb. butter, ½ pt. milk, 1 qt. molasses, 2 teaspoons saleratus, 2 tablespoons ginger. Make one day and bake the next.

Upper Shelf: 2 lbs. flour, ½ lb. butter, 3 eggs, ¾ lb. sugar, 1 nutmeg, ½ cup milk, 1 teaspoon saleratus. Add flour lastly and it will not usually require the full amount. Make one day and bake the next.

Jennie Dean's Heart-Cakes

Take 1 teacup sifted sugar, 1 teacup butter, 1 teaspoon cream, ½ teaspoon soda, 1 egg beaten light, and a little nutmeg. Flavor with extract of rose. Only sufficent flour to roll out the cakes *very* thin. Cut in hearts and bake.

> "To feed were best at home;
> From thence, the sauce to meat is ceremony;
> Meeting were bare without it."
> — MACBETH

Yule Cake

Take 1 lb. butter, 1 lb. sugar, 1½ lb. flour, 2 lbs. currants, ½ lb. citron, 1 lb. raisins, ¼ lb. orange and lemon peel (candied), 2 oz. almonds, ¼ oz. allspice, ¼ oz. cinnamon, 10 eggs, mace, nutmeg, clove. Melt the butter to a cream, beat in the sugar until light, adding the spices. In a quarter of an hour separate the eggs and work in yolks two at a time. Beat the whites to a stiff froth previously and add gradually to the mixture, which must not stand long enough to chill the butter else it will be heavy. Add to this the fruit and almonds, then the sifted flour and a glass of brandy. If baked in one cake it should be cooked slowly in a moderate oven about three hours.

> "Nearer as they came, a genial savour
> Of certain stews and roast meats and pilans,
> Things which in hungry mortals eyes find favour."
> — BYRON

What Salem Dames Cooked

Squash Pudding

1 qt. fine squash, 1 qt. milk or cream, 16 eggs, 1 lb. butter, 1¼ lbs. sugar, 2 nutmegs, 4 spoonfuls rose water, 2 to 4 groat biscuit.

MRS. DEVEREUX

Loaf Cake

2 lbs. flour, 1 lb. sugar, ¾ lb. butter, 6 eggs, 1 gill of wine, spice to your taste.

MISS LYDIA LEWIS (1808)

Johnny Cake

1 pint Indian meal, 1 cup flour stirred together; 1 pint of sour milk, into which put 1 teaspoon soda, 1 egg, little sugar, salt.

Mrs. Hoffman's Cakes

2½ lbs. flour, 1 lb. sugar, 1 lb. butter, 1 cup milk, 2 eggs, 1 tablespoon rose water, 1 teaspoon saleratus dissolved in little warm water, 1½ teaspoon ginger.

> "Come, Anthea, let us two
> Go to feast, as others do—
> Tarts and custards, creams and cakes
> Are the junkets still at wakes."
>
> HERRICK

Rose Cake

¾ lb. sugar, ½ lb. butter, 4 eggs, a little rose water, 1 lb. flour; spread with a knife as thin as possible on tins, bake a very light color, mark it in squares immediately on taking it out of the oven.

A RANTOUL RULE

Rice Cake

1 lb. sugar, ¾ lb. ground rice, 13 eggs, leaving out 4 of the whites, 1 spoonful salt, peel and juice of one lemon.

MRS. JOHONNOT

Our Grandmother's Cook Book

Spring Chicken *with* Cream Sauce

CUT up the chickens, roll in flour, pepper and salt them. Fry brown in boiling lard. When done thoroughly, take out and throw a little parsley in the pan to fry. Pour off all the lard, leaving all the parsley in the spider. One pint of sweet cream, salt and pepper it, and let it boil up. Pour over the chicken and save some to send to the table in a boat.

MRS. DONALDSON OF BALTIMORE

A Curry *from* London "Punch"

THREE pounds of veal my darling girl prepares
And chops it nicely into little squares.
Five onions next prepared the little minx,
The biggest are the best her Samivel thinks,
And Epping butter nearly half a pound
And stews them in a pan until they're browned.
What next my dexterous little girl will do?
She pops the meat into the savory stew
With curry powder tablespoonfuls three
And milk a pint, the richest that may be.
And when the dish has stewed for half an hour
A lemon's ready juice she'll o'er it pour.
Then, bless her—then she gives the luscious pot
A very gentle boil, and serves quite hot.   (1810)

Regent Sauce

1 qt. vinegar, 6 eschalots or 2 onions, 6 cloves pounded small, 4 tablespoons best mushroom catsup, 4 tablespoons soy, 1 tablespoon cayenne pepper. To stand ten days, shaking the bottle occasionally.

Batter Pudding

1 quart milk, 5 eggs, 8 tablespoons flour, a little salt. Boil it in a pudding pan or boiler. Eat with boiled molasses sauce to which is added a little butter and vinegar.

What Salem Dames Cooked

Mexican Tongue *with* Sauce

BOIL tongue until very tender, then skin, return to the water in which it has been boiled and let cool. Sauce: 1 cup sugar, 1 cup vinegar, 1 cup raisins stoned and halved, 1 lemon cut in dice form, 2 dozen whole cloves. When the tongue is cold put into a large pan and flour as for roasting. Pour sauce into the pan with tongue and cook half an hour, basting with the sauce three or four times.

> *"Some hae meat and canna eat*
> *And some hae nane that want it,*
> *But we hae meat and we can eat,*
> *Sae let the Lord be thankit."* — ROBERT BURNS

Muffins

2 lbs. flour, 1 qt. of milk, piece of butter as large as an egg, 4 teaspoons of yeast. Bake in a griddle or muffin rings. Do not cut them.

Sugar Gingerbread

2 lbs. flour, 1½ lbs. sugar, 1 lb. butter, 8 eggs, teacup full of ginger; make it very thin. Scrape it and sift sugar over it before putting in the oven. — MRS. LEVERETT SALTONSTALL

Blanc Mange

1 qt. milk, 1 oz. isinglass dissolved in water sufficient to cover it. Sugar, spice, and rose-water to taste. Let it boil up once. Strain through a thick bag and pour into moulds. In hot weather increase the quantity of isinglass.

— MRS. DUDLEY PICKMAN

Solid Syllabub

Mix a quart of thick cream, 1 lb. loaf sugar, ½ pint sweet wine in a deep pan. Put into it the peel and juice of three lemons, and beat or whisk it half an hour, then put it into glasses. — MRS. LEVERETT SALTONSTALL

Our Grandmother's Cook Book

Mary Lynde Brown's Coronation Pie

ROLL out six thin layers of the very best paste the size of a pie plate. Bake separately. When ready to serve, fill between the layers with delicate apple sauce seasoned with butter and lemon.

> "Though we eat little flesh and drink no wine
> Yet let's be merry: we'll have tea and toast;
> Custards for supper, and a luckless host
> Of syllabubs and jellies and mince pies
> And other such ladylike luxuries."
>
> — SHELLEY

Pandowdy

FILL a deep baking dish (old-fashioned bean pot) heaping full of sliced apples. Add 1 cup molasses, 1 cup sugar, 1 cup water, 1 teaspoon clove, 1 teaspoon cinnamon. Cover with a baking-powder biscuit crust, lapping it over the sides. Bake over night. In the morning cut the hard crust into the apple. Eat with cream or plain.

Blueberry Pudding

1 egg, ½ cup molasses, ½ teaspoon salt, ½ teaspoon soda, 1½ cups berries. Flour enough to make batter a little stiffer than for pound cake. Steam 1½ hours.

> "The proof of the pudding is in the eating." — CERVANTES

Mrs. Underwood's Fruit Cake

TAKE 4 cups flour, 3 cups sugar, 1½ cups butter, 1 cup milk, 4 eggs, 2 teaspoons clove, 2 teaspoons cinnamon, 1 nutmeg, 1 lb. raisins, 1 lb. currants, ½ cup molasses, ¼ lb. citron, ½ teaspoon soda. Bake three or four hours in a moderate oven. Keeps good for six months.

(*While eating the above, a guest at my grandmother's table was asked if he would have some bread, when he replied, "No, thank you, marm, I'm doing very well with this huckleberry gingerbread."*)

What Salem Dames Cooked

NIMBLE CAKE

TAKE ½ lb. of butter or lard rubbed with 1 lb. of flour. Mix rather soft with milk and add salt. Bake on tin sheets and cut in squares.   MRS. P. DEVEREUX

"Nimble cake for supper! How that sounds!
Go down to Mrs. Simons' and get some hearts and rounds."
  MISS M. DALRYMPLE, 1830

BRISTOL BANNOCKS

2 cups Indian meal, 1 cup flour, 1 large tablespoon molasses, 2 teaspoons baking powder. Mix well, add 1 egg and enough milk to soften. Drop from a spoon into very hot fat and fry.

PLUM PUDDING

TAKE 1 ¼ lbs. bread (baker's), ¾ lb. sugar, ½ lb. butter, 11 gills milk, 15 eggs, 2 lbs. stoned raisins, ½ lb. currants, ¼ lb. citron, 3 nutmegs, 2 glasses wine, teaspoonful saleratus dissolved in a little milk, salt to taste. The bread must have no crust. Grate all the bread. Put a layer of bread in the dish (having just buttered it), then a layer of butter cut up in small pieces, then a layer of raisins, currants and citron, till within two inches of the top of the dish. Take the sugar and eggs and beat up thoroughly with the milk; when well mixed add the nutmegs, wine, saleratus and salt to it. Then pour slowly into the dish, absorbing the bread gradually till all used up. Let it stand two or three hours before going into the oven. Bake about two hours.

SAUCE: To ½ gill wine, ½ gill rosewater, ½ lb. sugar, piece of butter as large as a good sized egg. Put it over a moderate fire and stir 15 minutes. When it has boiled up well, grate ½ nutmeg in the sauce boat and pour the sauce in. Four times this quantity will be needed for the pudding.
  MADAME PHILLIPS, 1790

"One solid dish his week-day meal affords
An added pudding solemnized the Lord's."
  POPE

FROM
Our Own Cook Books
1900

"Certainly," replied the oracle, "study the art of pleasing by dress and manner, and above all let all women, pretty and plain, married and single, study the art of cookery. If you are an artist in the kitchen, you will always be esteemed. Only be careful, in studying both arts, never to forget the great truth, that dinner precedes blandishments, and not blandishments, dinner."

ELIZABETH AND HER GERMAN GARDEN

STRAWBERRY PARFAIT

Box of strawberries crushed and strained; add 1½ cups of sugar, scant teaspoon of gelatine soaked in cold water or dissolved in a little hot water. Fold in ½ pint of whipped cream, sweeten and flavor with vanilla. Put in mould and pack with equal proportions of salt and ice. Let stand three hours.

CANTALOUPE FRAPPÉ

Select 2 large, ripe cantaloupes. Cut in halves, remove the seeds and scrape out the pulp. Press the pulp through a sieve to remove stringy portions. Add 1 cup powdered sugar and ½ cup orange juice. Season with a pinch of salt. Soak a tablespoon of gelatine in ¼ of a cup of water, set over boiling water and stir until dissolved. Stir this into the cantaloupe mixture, and when cold freeze slowly. Serve in sherbet glasses.

SPONGE CAKE

Weight of 6 eggs in sugar, weight of 3 eggs in flour, rind of 1 lemon and juice of ½ lemon. Beat yolks ten minutes and whites till stiff.

MRS. WM. SILSBEE

"For a man seldom thinks with more earnestness of anything than he does of his dinner."

SAMUEL JOHNSON

What Salem Dames Cooked

Custard Soufflé

CREAM 2 tablespoons butter, add 2 tablespoons flour, pour on gradually 1 cup of hot milk. Cook eight minutes in double boiler, stirring often. Separate the whites and yolks of 4 eggs. Put whites in ice chest. Beat yolks, add 2 tablespoons sugar to first mixture and set away to cool. Half an hour before serving beat the whites very stiff and cut them in lightly. Bake in a buttered pudding dish in a moderate oven thirty minutes. Serve at once with a creamy sauce flavored with sherry or strawberry.

Malaga Grape Salad

MAKE a French dressing with mustard, a spoonful of Worcestershire Sauce and a spoonful of horse-radish, with a trifle of sugar added to the usual ingredients. Cut grapes, carefully removing the seeds. Fill lettuce leaves and pour over the dressing. Both salad and dressing should be ice-cold when served.

"Oh herbacious treat!
'Twould tempt the dying anchorite to eat,
Back to the world he'd turn his fleeting soul
And plunge his fingers in the salad bowl." — SYDNEY SMITH

Jellied Pecan Salad

To 1 pt. of lemon jelly, when nearly hard, add 1 cup of broken pecan meats; mold in wine glasses and serve on lettuce leaves with finely shaved green peppers and mayonnaise.

"To speak of salads in aught but the most reverential spirit were sacrilege."
— E. R. PENNELL

Peanut Soup

1 qt. milk, 1 qt. peanuts, 1 slice onion; chop nuts very fine, put them with the onion in the milk, boil three-quarters of an hour, thicken with 1 teaspoon flour, small piece of butter, salt, and serve.

Our Own Cook Books

RICE CURRY—ZANZIBAR CURRY

MIX 2 tablespoons flour and 2 tablespoons curry powder with water enough to make it a paste. Put a pint of water in the frying pan, add the flour, and boil until quite thick. Then add 2 spoonfuls of the gravy. Slice the meat, cold lamb, beef or chicken, with the fat taken off, and boil just enough to warm the meat. Slice two hard boiled eggs and put around the dish.

THIN SUGAR GINGERBREAD

1 cup butter, 2 cups sugar, a little soda in sugar, 1 teaspoon ginger, 3 eggs; enough flour to roll out. Spread with knife on tins, and sprinkle sugar on just as it goes into the oven.

MISS S. E. OSGOOD

TURMERIC GINGERBREAD

2 cups sugar, ⅔ cup butter, 1 cup milk, 4 eggs, 2 teaspoons cream tartar, 1 teaspoon soda, 2 large tablespoons turmeric ginger, 2½ cups flour.

A. L. A.

ASPARAGUS SOUP

TO 3 cups of cooked asparagus (may use canned), add 2 slices onion, ½ cup boiling water, 1 qt. chicken or veal broth, ¼ cup butter, ¼ cup flour, ½ teaspoon of salt and paprika, 2 cups milk. Cook the first three ingredients until the water has nearly evaporated. Press through a sieve, add the broth. Make a white sauce of the remaining ingredients. When ready to serve, combine the two mixtures by gradually stirring the asparagus into the white sauce.

STRAWBERRY ICE CREAM

2 qts. of strawberries covered with 2 cups of sugar and left over night, or at least four or five hours. Mash and strain berries, then add 1 qt. of cream and freeze.

What Salem Dames Cooked

BOILED DRESSING *for* COLD SLAW

BOIL ½ cup sugar, ½ teaspoon each of salt, mustard and pepper. Rub ¼ cup of butter to a cream with 1 teaspoon of flour, and pour the boiling vinegar on it. Cook five minutes, then pour it over a well-beaten egg. Mix this dressing while hot with one pint of shaved cabbage or a mixed vegetable salad.

MINCE *for* PIES

TAKE 10 lbs. of beef, which will make 4 lbs. when chopped, 3 lbs. suet, 4 lbs. apples, 2 lbs. citron, 4 lbs. brown sugar, 4 spoonfuls salt, 4 lbs. raisins, 4 lbs. currants; pint of wine, gill of brandy, 5 nutmegs, 1 tablespoon clove, 2 tablespoons cinnamon, 3 lemons.   MISS SUSAN OSGOOD

MINT JELLY

WASH 3 qts. of grapes, fully grown but entirely green, and put these over the fire with three pints of boiling water. Cook 15 minutes, breaking and mashing them with a wooden spoon; turn into a jelly bag and strain. Measure the juice and return it to the fire, adding sprigs of freshly bruised spearmint; boil for 20 minutes, skim, removing the mint, and for each cup of juice add 1 scant cup of sugar which has been made hot in the oven. Stir until it boils up, which will be almost instantly; remove any froth that rises and it is ready to pour into glasses. The color will be pale, greenish amber. A suspicion of coloring paste makes it a delicate mint green. This is especially choice to serve with lamb.

CRANBERRY PUNCH

COOK 1½ qts. of cranberries in 1½ qts. of water till they have popped. Then strain and add a syrup made by boiling 2 cups of sugar and 1 cup of water together 10 minutes and then adding the juice of 4 lemons. Dilute to taste.

Our Own Cook Books

Nantucket Scallops Chowder

TAKE 4 medium sized potatoes, 4 slices salt pork, ½ small onion sliced, 3 pts. sweet milk, 1 qt. scallops (if large cut in two or more pieces), 4 Marblehead hard crackers. Peel and slice potatoes, parboil in a little salted water until nearly soft. Place the pork and onion in a frying pan, cook until the onion is a deep, rich brown color; remove scraps of pork and onion and place this gravy in a fairly large stew pan, and add a portion of the milk. When quite hot, add the potatoes; cook a short time, then add the scallops, with a little salt, pepper, and a dash of good cayenne pepper; this latter is quite important. Mix a scant tablespoon of flour or corn starch in with a little cold milk; add this to the chowder and cook a short time longer. Place the opened crackers in a tureen, having soaked them in cold water; pour the chowder over them and serve.

> "*The chowder on the sand beach made*
> *Dipped by the hungry, steaming hot,*
> *With spoons of clam-shells from the pot.*" — WHITTIER

Currant Conserve

5 qts. currants, 5 lbs. sugar, 1 qt. red raspberries; juice of 6 oranges and pulp and peel of one cut into small pieces, 2 lbs. seeded raisins. Put all together and boil very slowly until it jellies.

Cranberry Pudding

Cream ½ cup of butter, add slowly 1 cup sugar, 3 eggs well beaten; 2 teaspoons cream tartar sifted into 3½ cups flour. Add to the first mixture 1 cup milk, 1 teaspoon soda. Stir in lightly 2 cups cranberries and steam two hours. To be served with any sweet sauce.

> "*He who is not conscious of pleasure when he eats is not worthy to sit at table with the elect.*" — E. R. PENNELL

What Salem Dames Cooked

Welsh Rarebit

TAKE 1 teaspoon butter, ¼ to ½ lb. cheese cut in small pieces, ¼ teaspoon salt, ¼ teaspoon mustard, few grains cayenne, ½ cup thin cream or rich milk, 1 egg. Toast or crackers. Melt butter, add cheese and seasonings; as cheese melts add the cream gradually, stirring constantly, then the egg slightly beaten. Cook slowly till thickened. May use ⅓ to ½ cup ale or lager in place of the cream.

A Summer Drink

Let stand for some hours lemons, sugar and fresh mint; 2 lemons to each bottle of ginger ale. Pour the ale on to the lemons and sugar when needed for use. Should be very cold.

> *Drink now the strong beer,*
> *Cut the white loaf here,*
> *The while the meat is a-shredding,*
> *For the rare mince-pie*
> *And the plums stand by*
> *To fill the paste that's a-kneading."*
>
> — HERRICK

Pistachio Cream *and* Peaches

TAKE 1 pt. milk, 1 tablespoon flour, 1 cup sugar, 1 egg, 1 pt. cream, 1 tablespoon vanilla, 1 teaspoon almond, Burnett's green coloring, chilled fresh peaches. Cook first three ingredients in double boiler 15 minutes, then add egg and cook 10 minutes longer. Cool and add the cream, vanilla, almond, and enough coloring to make a pale green. Freeze and serve with chilled fresh peaches peeled, halved, and the centres filled with chopped walnuts.

To Clean Brass

Plain, not lacquered or burnished: If stained, rub with a solution of oxalic acid. Wash off thoroughly and quickly with soap and water. Polish with whiting; for the oil, use sweet, cottonseed or kerosene. Dust every week with oiled cloth.

Our Own Cook Books

STUFFED PEPPERS

SPLIT 4 sweet bell peppers in halves lengthwise. Remove seeds and ribs. Prepare a stuffing as follows: 1½ cups stale bread crumbs, 1 small onion grated, tomato freshly stewed, or canned, to moisten. Season highly with salt, pepper and paprika. Mix lightly and fill the peppers. Put a small lump of butter on each and bake ½ to ¾ of an hour in a hot oven, with a little water in the pan.

"Get me twenty cunning cooks."   ROMEO AND JULIET

CREAM CAKES

TAKE 1 pt. water, ½ lb. butter, 1 lb. flour, 10 eggs. Follow the directions implicitly and delicious cream cakes will be the result. Boil the butter and water together, and stir in the flour while boiling. Take it from the fire to cool, when cool *stir* in the eggs one at a time. *Don't beat.* Stir thoroughly, add 1 teaspoon of cold water. Drop into pans. Have the oven quite hot and avoid opening it. Bake about 15 minutes. Open cakes at the side and fill with this mixture: 1 cup flour, 2 cups sugar, 4 eggs, 1 qt. milk. Boil milk, beat eggs, flour and sugar together, stir them into the milk while boiling until thickened well. Add lemon when cool and fill the cakes.

"Heaven sends us good meat, but the devil sends us cooks."
    GOLDSMITH

BROWNIES

TAKE ½ cup butter, 1 cup sugar, ½ cup flour, 2 eggs, 2 squares melted chocolate, ½ or 1 cup chopped walnuts. Cream butter and sugar, add eggs and flour. Mix all together and add chocolate. Bake in dripping pan and cut into shape while warm.

For Cleaning Greasy Frying Pans

Use first a soft paper, newspaper will do, but tissue is better.

What Salem Dames Cooked

Brandy Snaps

Take 1 cup butter, 2 cups P. O. molasses, boil together ½ hour; add ⅓ cup flour, ⅔ cup cocoanut, 1 even teaspoon soda. Boil ten minutes, stirring constantly. Drop in small lumps on a buttered tin and bake gently till they bubble. Let stand a minute or two, then slip a knife under and lay them flat on a cold tin.

"Like as my parlour so my hall
  and kitchen's small,
A little buttery, and therein
  a little bin,
Which keeps my little loaf of bread
  unshipped, unflead;
Lord I confess too, when I dine
  the pulse is thine,
And all those other bits that be
  there placed by Thee." — HERRICK

Orange Cake

Cream ¼ cup butter, add gradually 1 cup sugar; beat 3 eggs separately, 1 ⅔ cup pastry flour, 2 level teaspoons baking powder. Add the flour to the mixture alternately with ½ cup milk. Bake in a shallow pan, cut in halves, or in a deeper one and split.

Filling: Mix in order given ½ cup sugar, 1 generous tablespoon bread flour, grated rind of ½ orange, ¼ cup orange juice, ½ tablespoon lemon juice, 1 egg, 1 teaspoon butter. Cook in double boiler ten minutes. When cold, spread between cakes.

Frosting: Grated rind of 1 orange, cover with 1 teaspoon brandy, ½ teaspoon lemon juice. Let stand twenty minutes. Strain and add gradually the yolk of 1 egg and confectioner's sugar until the right consistency to spread on cake.

Care of Dover Egg-beater
Do not put cogs of beater in water. Oil occasionally.

SUPRÉME OF CHICKEN

CHOP very fine the breast of a raw chicken, and beat into it one at a time 4 eggs and ½ pint cream. Season with salt and pepper. Butter small moulds, fill with chicken mixture, and bake standing in hot water covered with a buttered paper twenty minutes. Do not let the water boil. Serve with bechamel or mushroom sauce.

*"Serenely full, the epicure would say,
'Fate cannot harm me, I have dined to-day.'"*

SYDNEY SMITH

CARAWAY LOAF CAKE

1 lb. flour, ½ lb. sugar, 5 oz. butter, 4 eggs, 1 cup milk, 1 small spoonful saleratus, 1 tablespoon caraway seeds.

MISS BARKER, NO. ANDOVER

QUEEN'S CAKE

½ lb. butter (with a heavy hand), 1 lb. flour, 1 lb. sugar, 1 cup milk, 5 eggs, 1 grain nutmeg.

MISS S. E. OSGOOD

*"I sing the sweets I know, the charms I feel—
My morning incense, and my evening meal,
The sweets of hasty pudding."*

BARLOW

CHEESE CAKES

Line baking cups with nice pie-crust. Fill with Queen's cake mixture, putting strips of pastry across top and bake.

RAISED WAFFLES

SCALD 1¾ cup milk, pour it over 1 teaspoon salt, add 1 tablespoon butter, ½ yeast cake dissolved in ¼ cup lukewarm water, 2 cups pastry flour. Beat with Dover beater until smooth. Let rise, then add 2 eggs beaten separately. Cook in waffle iron.

What Salem Dames Cooked

OMELETTE

TAKE 3 eggs, ½ cup milk, 1 teaspoon butter, 1 *even* tablespoon flour. Beat yolks of eggs light; warm the milk and dissolve butter in it. Mix yolks, flour, milk and butter well together; lastly the whites of the eggs beaten to a stiff froth. Pour into a hot buttered pan, season with salt and pepper over the top; cook covered a few minutes on hot part of stove, then remove to cooler part of stove to finish. Fold and serve. (The recipe of a Georgia colored cook famous for her delicious omelettes.)

> *"Thou mak'st my teeming hen to lay*
> *Her egg each day."* — HERRICK

ENGLISH SWEET-BREAD

1 pt. of hot milk poured on a cup of butter, 1 cup of sugar, a little salt. When cool, add ½ yeast cake. Flour for soft mould; currants or carraway seeds as desired. Rise 3 times, stirring down dough between times.

MAPLE CREAMS

1 cup rich cream, 2 cups maple sugar. Boil until it is on the point of spinning a thread. Cool and beat until creamy; add chopped walnuts and pour into a well-buttered pan. Cut in squares when partially hardened.

YELLOW TOMATO PRESERVE

TAKE 3 lbs. small yellow tomatoes, 3 lbs. sugar, ¼ lb. green ginger, 2 lemons sliced very thin. Make a syrup of the sugar with a very little water, drop in tomatoes, ginger and lemon. Have the tomatoes skinned or not, as you please. Boil very slowly until syrup jellies. It is well to let it stand over night in a kettle; if not thick enough, put on the fire again in the morning.

Our Own Cook Books

OYSTER COCKTAILS

TAKE 7 teaspoons tomato catsup, 7 teaspoons horse-radish, 10 teaspoons lemon juice, 1 teaspoon tobasco sauce, salt. Enough sauce for six persons. Keep oysters in towel on ice until very cold. Use small oysters. Fill cocktail glasses with oysters and cover with sauce.

> *"Epicurean cooks*
> *Sharpen with cloyless sauce his appetite."*
> ANTONY AND CLEOPATRA

CITRON MELON

PEEL the melon, take out the inside, and cut it in small pieces. Weigh the melon and use same weight of sugar. Put the melon to boil in water enough to cover it, boil until tender. Take it up in a dish, sprinkle the sugar over it, and let it remain over night. In the morning pour off the syrup, and boil until clarified. Then put the melon in and boil until scalded through; place in a dish to cool. Add to the syrup lemons and preserved ginger; boil syrup again until quite clear. Put the melon in jars and turn the syrup over it hot. Use 6 lemons to 5 lbs. of melon.

> *"Herbs, and other country messes*
> *Which the neat-handed Phyllis dresses."*
> MILTON

MUSTARD PICKLE

TAKE 1 cauliflower, 1 bunch celery, 1 qt. small white onions, 100 small cucumbers, 1 qt. green tomatoes. Cut coarsely the tomatoes and celery, break cauliflower into small pieces; onions and cucumbers to be left whole. Add 4 qts. water, 1 pt. salt. Let it stand 24 hours.

DRESSING: 1 cup flour, 2 cups sugar, 2 qts. vinegar, 5 tablespoons mustard, 1 tablespoon turmeric. Turn this over the pickle and cook slowly until soft.

What Salem Dames Cooked

Scotch Short Bread

TAKE ½ lb. butter, 1 lb. pastry flour, ¼ lb. sugar. Wash the butter to remove salt, cream it and the sugar very thoroughly, add the flour gradually. Shape into small round cakes, or sheets an inch thick. Bake in very moderate oven a delicate brown. When cool sprinkle with confectioner's sugar.

"Where's the cook? Is supper ready?
The house trimmed, rushes strewed, cobwebs swept?"
TAMING OF THE SHREW

Orange Balls

Yolk of one egg. Rind and juice of one orange. Confectioner's sugar sufficient to make the mixture stiff. Make into little balls and roll in granulated sugar. A teaspoonful of brandy or Jamaica rum is an improvement.

Pineapple Sherbet

BOIL 3 cups of water, 1 pint of sugar and 1 pt. of fresh pineapple cut in pieces together 15 minutes. Add 1 teaspoon gelatine softened in 1 tablespoon cold water. When cold add juice of 2 lemons and 1 cup cream beaten stiff, and then freeze. The cream may be omitted if not desired.

"Let vapid idlers loll in silk
Around their costly board;
Give us the bowl of samp and milk
By homespun beauty poured."
WHITTIER

Devonshire Clotted Cream

LET milk stand 24 hours in winter and 12 hours in summer. Then heat *very slowly* on the back of range until it wrinkles and bubbles. Set it aside in a cool place for some length of time. Skim and serve with fresh fruit jams or preserves.

Our Own Cook Books

Mushroom Consommé

WHEN cooking fresh mushrooms, save the peel and stems. Chop them fine and keep them dry in a cool place in a covered jar. Make ordinary consommé, only chop the vegetables fine and sauté in butter before adding to the stock. Clear and strain the stock, then add 1 tablespoon of the mushroom powder to 6 cups consommé. Serve with a tablespoon of whipped cream in each cup.

> *"If we can meet and so confer*
> *Both by a shining salt-cellar—*
> *We'll eat our bean with that full mirth*
> *As we were lords of all the earth."*
>
> HERRICK

Symbals

2½ lbs. flour, 1 ¼ lbs. sugar, 6 oz. butter, 10 eggs, 2 spoonfuls wine, spice. Have the lard very hot for frying, but not so hot as to burn or scorch.

MRS. S. PICKERING

Sally Lund (*Tea Cake*)

1 qt. flour, 2 eggs, 1 pt. milk, butter size of an egg, ½ teacup sugar, ½ teaspoon salt, 2 teaspoons cream tartar, 1 teaspoon soda. Bake in shallow pans and cut in squares.

MRS. FRANKLIN STORY

Iron Clads

TAKE 1 cup cold water, 1 cup milk, 2 cups flour. Put water and milk together. Stir flour into half of it until smooth, then add the rest and beat very light with egg beater. Have iron muffin pan so hot that it smokes when butter is put into it. Pour in one cooking spoon of batter for each muffin. Bake fifteen minutes in very hot oven. Should be thin, hollow and crisp when done.

> *"Of right choice food are his meals."* DICKENS

What Salem Dames Cooked

Marshmallow Pudding

SOAK ¼ cup candied cherries in rum to cover for one hour; cut in pieces and add to ½ cup walnut meats and ⅛ lb. marshmallows also cut in pieces. Whip 1 cup heavy cream; add 2 tablespoons powdered sugar and ½ teaspoon vanilla, and fold this into the other ingredients. Mould and chill.

Tea Punch

TAKE 1 doz. lemons, 1 small pineapple, about 1 qt. of tea (half Ceylon and half Oolong), some sprigs of mint. Squeeze lemons and cut pineapple into small dice. Add about 3 cups of sugar and let it stand over night. Cover the lemon rinds with cold water. In the morning squeeze the rinds again; add all the water to the mixture, and next the freshly made tea. Sugar to taste, and dilute with 1 qt. or more of water. Before serving add ice and mint.

> *"They eat, they drink, and in communion sweet*
> *Quaff immortality and joy."* — MILTON

Floating Pudding

STIR into 1 qt. boiling milk, 3 tablespoons flour beaten into 4 eggs, a little salt. Let boil ten minutes. Put into a dish and pour over it while hot a cup of sugar. Before going to the table add a glass of wine.

Salem Cup Cake

TAKE 1½ cup butter, 3 cups sugar, 5 eggs, 1½ cup milk, 4½ even teaspoons baking powder, 4½ cups pastry flour, lemon and nutmeg. Cream butter, add sugar, yolks of eggs well beaten and milk. Add flour gradually, with baking powder sifted into flour; add flavoring. Beat well, then fold in the stiffly beaten whites of eggs. Bake in moderate oven.

Our Own Cook Books

CREAMED SHAD ROE

PARBOIL one large or two small shad roes in slightly acidulated water for twenty minutes. Remove the membrane and mash. Make a cream by melting 3 tablespoons of butter cooked for five minutes with 1 teaspoon finely minced shallot; add 1½ tablespoon flour, ¼ teaspoon salt, a generous sprinkling of pepper; then add ½ cup cream and the yolks of 2 eggs slightly beaten and the juice of 1 lemon; add the roe. Spread thin buttered toast with the creamed roe. Garnish with cress and slices of lemon.

"A fat kitchen maketh a lean will." —BENJ. FRANKLIN

PRESERVED PEACHES

PEEL ripe perfect peaches and pack them closely in jars. Prepare a rich syrup in the proportion of a pint of water to 4 lbs. of sugar, and pour it when boiling hot over the peaches, taking care to fill every crevice in the jars, and to the *brim*. Screw on the covers tightly and stand them in a boiler full of boiling water. Cover with a blanket to keep the water hot as long as possible. Remove the jars when the water is cold. Screw covers tight. Keep in a dark, cool place.

CHOCOLATE CAKE

TAKE 1 oz. chocolate, ½ cup butter, 1½ cup sugar, 4 eggs, ½ cup milk, 1¾ cup pastry flour, 1 heaping teaspoon baking powder, vanilla. Dissolve chocolate, then add 5 tablespoons boiling water. Cream butter and sugar, add yolks, stir well, add a little of the milk. Beat whites of eggs stiff. Take beater from stiff whites and put into butter, sugar, yolks, etc., and beat until very light. Add the rest of milk, vanilla and chocolate. Fold in flour to which has been added baking powder. Lastly add the stiff whites of eggs. Bake forty-five minutes.

What Salem Dames Cooked

Fruit Puff Pudding

INTO 1 pt. of flour stir 2 teaspoons baking powder and a pinch of salt; beat 1 egg and add enough milk to make into a very soft dough. Place well buttered tins in a steamer and into each put 1 spoonful of dough, then a spoonful of strawberries mashed with sugar, and cover with a little more of the dough. Steam twenty minutes and serve with this sauce: 2 eggs, ½ cup butter, 1 cup sugar, beaten thoroughly; then add 1 cup boiling milk, and just before serving 1 cup of crushed strawberries.

"In the planning of the perfect meal there is Art."   E. R. PENNELL

Dandelion Wine

TAKE 2 qts. of blossoms picked from stem. Pour over this 4 qts. boiling water and let stand three days, stirring each day. Strain and add 5 lbs. sugar, 3 oranges and 3 lemons sliced very thin, 1 yeast cake dissolved in water. Let stand three days more, strain; let stand four weeks, strain, and add ½ pint whiskey. Put 3 raisins in each bottle.

Cream Griddle Cakes

1 pt. cream whipped, yolks 4 eggs, 2 tablespoons sugar, ½ cup flour. Beat the whites of eggs till stiff and add after the flour. Bake on griddle at once.

Maple Sugar Ice Cream

To a scant cup of rich maple syrup add beaten yolks of 4 eggs and cook, stirring until it boils. Strain through sieve and cool. Beat 1 pt. cream, add beaten whites, and whip syrup until light. Mix together and freeze.

To Remove Stains from Kitchen Utensils

For tin, use Bon Ami.   For agate ware, use Sapolio.
For knives, use bath brick.

Our Own Cook Books

ORANGE SOUP

Squeeze sufficient oranges to make a quart of juice drained. Strain and place over the fire. Add ½ cup sugar; moisten 2 tablespoons arrowroot. When the juice reaches the boiling point, add the arrowroot. Stir for a moment, take from the fire, and when cool add 2 tablespoons curaçoa cordial. When ready to serve, put into your punch glasses a few small pieces of ice; have the soup cold before pouring into the glasses.

SAUCE NORVEGIENNE *for Boiled Fish*

Whip ½ pt. cream and add 3 tablespoons mayonnaise, 1 teaspoon English mustard (mixed), 1½ tablespoon bottled horseradish, salt and cayenne pepper. Serve sauce ice cold, keep it surrounded with ice until served.

*"O hour, of all hours the most blessed upon earth,
Blessed hour of our dinners."* — OWEN MEREDITH

HERMITS

1 cup butter, 1½ cup sugar, 3 eggs well beaten, 1 teaspoon cloves, 1 teaspoon cassia, 1 teaspoon mace, 1 teaspoon soda, 1 cup stoned raisins chopped fine. Mix very hard with sufficient flour to roll very thin.

ORANGE *or* GRAPE-FRUIT PEEL

Use only thick peel. Cut in long, narrow pieces. Soak over night in cold water to which has been added salt, perhaps a handful. In morning wash, put in cold water, and boil one hour. Pour off water and boil again in fresh cold water until the peel can be pierced easily with a broom straw. Drain and pour over this a syrup made of 3 cups water and 3 cups sugar. Boil until syrup has disappeared. When cool enough roll the peel in sugar.

𝔚hat 𝔖alem 𝔇ames 𝔠ooked

BUCKWHEAT CAKES

TAKE 1 qt. buckwheat flour, 2 tablespoons yeast, a little salt, and about 1 qt. of warm water (as warm as new milk). Let stand over night in a pretty warm place, as you would put bread to rise. In the morning dissolve ½ teaspoon or 1 teaspoon soda (according to how much batter is risen) in 1 tablespoon of milk, and stir it in. Be sure to mix the cakes thin and brown on both sides. (An excellent recipe.)

ALMOND CREAM SOUP

TAKE 1 qt. rich veal stock, 1 pt. cream, 2 tablespoons butter, 2 tablespoons flour, 1 tablespoon chopped onion, ¼ lb. shelled almonds, ½ teaspoon white pepper, 2 teaspoons salt, bit of mace, thin yellow rind of lemon. Blanch almonds and pound to a paste in a mortar, adding a tablespoon of water from time to time to keep the almonds from becoming oily. Put the butter in a saucepan and when it is melted add the onion; cook for five minutes, being careful not to brown. Add the flour to the butter and onion and stir over the fire until frothy but not brown. Gradually add the stock, stirring all the time. When this boils add the salt, pepper, mace and lemon peel. Simmer twenty minutes. Put the cream and almonds in a double boiler over the fire. Cook for fifteen minutes, then strain the contents of the stew pan into this, stirring all the time. Cook five minutes longer and strain through a fine purée strainer.

FRENCH CHESTNUTS ON TOAST

GASH the shells of the chestnuts and boil until soft (about twenty minutes), then peel and put in spider to brown with a piece of butter the size of a walnut, a teaspoon of sugar, a pinch of salt, (no pepper), and stir with a fork until brown. Then serve on hot pieces of toast.

"Eat at your own table as you would at the table of the King." CONFUCIUS

INDEX

	PAGE		PAGE
A Bill of Fare for Midsomer	7	Dandelion Wine	36
A Most Pleasant Drink	10	Darbyshire Pudding	11
Another	10	Devonshire Clotted Cream	32
Almond Cream Soup	38	Election Cake	14
Apple Fritters	12	English Hunting Beef	13
Asparagus Soup	23	English Sweet-bread	30
A Summer Drink	26	Floating Pudding	34
Bannuch Cakes	12	Fruit Puff Pudding	36
Batter Pudding	17	French Chestnuts on Toast	38
Blanc Mange	18	Good Wigs, *To make*	9
Blueberry Pudding	19	Hedg-hog Pudding, *To make a*	7
Boiled Dressing	24	Hermits	37
Brandy Snaps	28		
Breast of Mutton, *To carbonade a*	9	Iron Clads	33
Bristol Bannocks	20	Jellied Pecan Salad	22
Brownies	27	Jennie Dean's Heart Cakes	15
Buckwheat Cakes	38	Johnny Cake	16
Burnt Cream	9	Loaf Cake	16
Cantaloupe Frappé	21	Malaga Grape Salad	22
Caraway Loaf Cake	29	Maple Creams	30
Cheese Cakes	29	Maple Sugar Ice Cream	36
Chicken-Pye, *To make a*	7	Marshmallow Pudding	34
Chocolate Cake	35	Mary Lynde's Coronation Pie	19
Citron Melon	31	Meg Merrilies Pottage	12
Corn Pone	13	Mexican Tongue	18
Cranberry Pudding	25	Mince for Pies	24
Cranberry Punch	24	Mint Jelly	24
Cream Cakes	27	Molly Saunders' Gingerbread	15
Cream Griddle Cakes	36	Mrs. Hoffman's Cake	16
Creamed Shad Roe	35	Mrs. Underwood's Fruit Cake	19
Currant Conserve	25	Muffins	18
Curry, *from London Punch*	17	Mushroom Consommé	33
Custard Soufflé	22	Mustard Pickle	31

Index

	PAGE		PAGE
Nantucket Scallops Chowder	25	Salem Pudding	14
Nimble Cake	20	Sally Lund	33
Omelette	30	Sauce Norvegienne for Boiled Fish	37
Orangado Pie, *To make an*	8	Scotch Short-bread	32
Orange Balls	32	Shrewsbury Cakes	10
Orange Cake	28	Solid Syllabub	18
Orange or Grape-Fruit Peel	37	Sponge Cake	21
Orange Soup	37	Spring Chicken with Cream Sauce	17
Oyster Cocktails	31	Squash Pudding	16
Pandowdy	19	Strawberry Ice Cream	23
Panola, *For the sick*	10	Strawberry Parfait	21
Peanut Soup	22	Stuffed Peppers	27
Pineapple Sherbet	32	Sugar Gingerbread	18
Pistachio Cream and Peaches	26	Supréme of Chicken	29
Plum Pudding	20	Symbals	33
Pound Cake	11		
Preserved Peaches	35	Tea Punch	34
Pye with Pippins, *To make a*	8	Thin Sugar Gingerbread	23
Queen's Cake	29	Trifle, *To make a*	11
Raised Waffles	29	Turmeric Gingerbread	23
Regent Sauce	17	Typical Prices	8
Rice Cake	16	Wedding Cake	14
Rice Curry—Zanzibar Curry	23	Welsh Rarebit	26
Rose Cake	16	Whip Syllabub	14
Rules for		White Currant Shrub	12
Caring for Kitchen Utensils	36		
Cleaning Dover Egg-beater	28	Yellow Gingerbread	13
Cleaning Brass	26	Yellow Tomato Preserve	30
Cleaning Greasy Frying Pans	27	Yule Cake	15
Salem Cup Cake	34	Zanzibar Gingerbread	14

WHAT
𝔖alem 𝔇ames
COOKED

What Salem Dames Cooked
Original Published in 1910
The Stetson Press of Boston
for the Esther C. Mack Industrial School
Salem, Massachusetts

ISBN 978-1-7335937-0-0

DERBY SQUARE PRESS is the publishing house
of Wicked Good Books, the independent bookstore in Salem, MA.

The mission of Derby Square Press
is to find and once again make available to the public
out of print books of historical significance.

This book is a copy of the original.

Due to its age, it may contain imperfections
such as marks or flawed pages
but at the same time is a modern edition reflecting the original work.

www.ingramcontent.com/pod-product-compliance
Lightning Source LLC
Chambersburg PA
CBHW021639080526
44584CB00015BA/1594